Endorsements

The Hammer of Hope is such a sweet way of sharing important stories from the Bible and tying them all together with the common theme of the hammer. Children will love the colorful illustrations that bring the story to life. This has such a great message that will truly resonate with young readers!

–**KATY NEWTON NASS**, Author of *Guardian*, Gold Book Award Recipient 2017

Nothing, no matter how insignificant, is wasted in God's story. Katie Hook captures the role of a simple hammer in the flood story and in the Gospel story. She reminds us that our lives are His tool to bring hope of the Gospel to the world.

–**IVA MAY**, founder and director of Chronological Bible Teaching Ministries

In *The Hammer of Hope*, Katie Hook shares the gospel message in a way kids will understand. Her rhythmic words mimic the subtle beat of a simple hammer building faithfulness and hope in people's lives. I could see this book becoming a family's favorite read-a-long story.

–**KRISTIN HILL TAYLOR**, author of *Peace in the Process: How Adoption Built My Faith & My Family*

The Hammer of Hope

Published in New York, New York, by Morgan James Publishing. Morgan James is a trademark of Morgan James, LLC. www.MorganJamesPublishing.com

ISBN 9781642793239 paperback
ISBN 9781642793246 eBook
Library of Congress Control Number: 2018912415

Cover and Interior Design by:
Chris Treccani
www.3dogcreative.net

Morgan James is a proud partner of Habitat for Humanity Peninsula and Greater Williamsburg. Partners in building since 2006.

Get involved today! Visit
MorganJamesPublishing.com/giving-back

The Hammer of HOPE

Written by
Katie Hook

Illustrated by
Nathan Corbit

NEW YORK

LONDON • NASHVILLE • MELBOURNE • VANCOUVER

Bang. Bang. Bang. Noah swung his hammer high into the air.
Sweat trickled down his face; the pain was hard to bear.
The hammer drove the nails deep into the wood
And held the ship together just like God said it would.

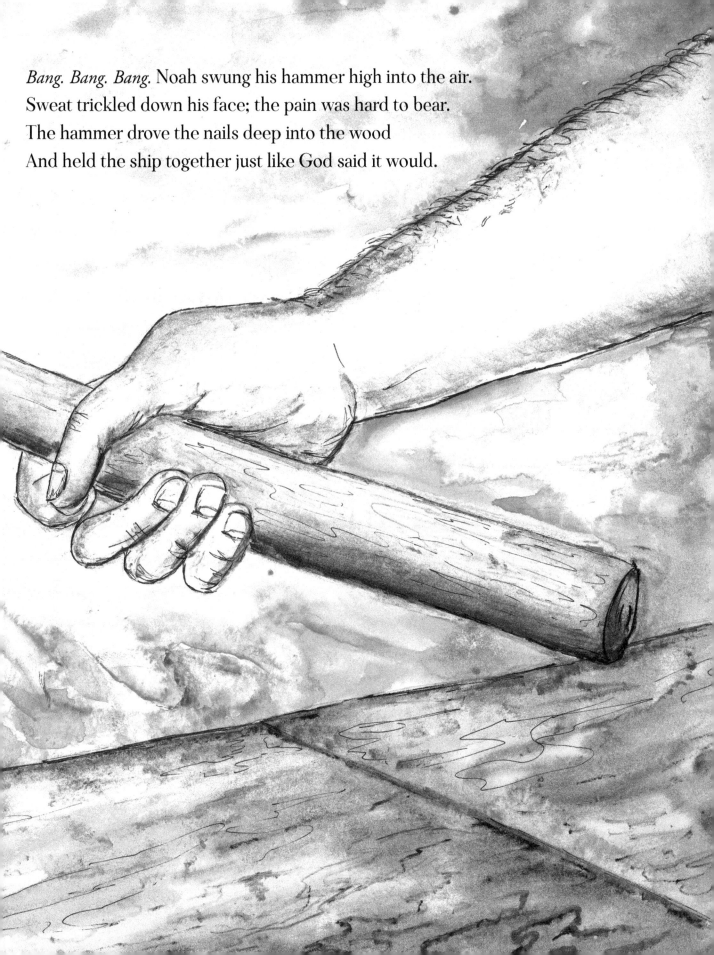

Noah and his family obeyed the word God had given.
They built the ship, and because of their decision
People mocked them and put their faith to the test.
After 120 years the ark was built and they could finally rest.

Noah loved the people and told them about the flood,
But they refused to listen—Noah's warnings weren't enough.
But the animals miraculously came and climbed upon the ship;
Two of every kind arrived and no one even used a whip.

God shut the door of the ark with a loud and thunderous boom.
The people who made fun of Noah began to see their doom.
Noah felt the first raindrop splash and trickle down his face.
Forty days and nights it rained—yet God saved them by His grace.

The hammer was just a simple tool Noah used to build the ark,
And when Noah swung it, the clanging created a spark.
The light of God's love shone through Noah and the hammer.
Who knew a simple tool and a common man could make such a clamor?

We are like that hammer—a part in the story God has planned,
Shining light into this world while placed in His everlasting hand.
We can't do it on our own. He helps us swing with might.
Trusting Him is our only hope to make this world shine bright.

Bang. Bang. Bang. Joseph swung the hammer high above his head.
This carpenter from Nazareth built tables, chairs, and beds.
His wages helped him feed his growing family with great joy.
He and his wife Mary knew Jesus was a very special boy.

Joseph had a dream about Jesus even before His birth.
An angel said, "Don't be afraid. God is sending a Baby to earth."
Joseph sure had a big job. How hard it must have been!
But he knew God was watching over every one of them.

Joseph chiseled the wood and sanded it smooth.
Boy Jesus worked with him and learned carpentry too.
And whenever Jesus spoke, Joseph heard God's voice.
He knew without a doubt Jesus was no ordinary boy.

The hammer was just a simple tool used by Joseph to do God's will.

When Joseph swung the hammer, God's words were being fulfilled.

The light of God's love shone through Joseph and the hammer.

Who knew such a simple tool and a common man could make such a clamor?

We are like a hammer—a part in the story God has planned,
Shining light into this world while placed in His everlasting hand.
We can't do it on our own. He helps us swing with might.
Trusting Jesus is our only hope to make this world shine bright.

Bang! Bang! Bang! The Roman soldiers swung their hammers high into the air.

Sweat trickled down Jesus' face; the pain was hard to bear.

The hammer drove the nails deep into His feet and hands.

They held the Son of God on the cross—it was heard across the lands.

Jesus had to die, you see, so we could be born again.
His cruel death was all part of God's redemption plan.
He didn't stay upon that cross but rose alive from the grave.
The nations all around the world are who He came to save.

Jesus is a friend who sticks closer than a brother.
He wants us to love him and to also love each other.
Simply bow your head and think of all the creation He has made.
Now thank Him for all He's done and the huge cost that He paid.

When we love Jesus, we want to tell everyone we know.
Loving one another is the way He wants us to grow.
Life on earth can be such a joy when we know Jesus as our Lord.
Heaven is waiting once we leave this earth— as we walk forward.

The hammer was just a simple tool used to save the world.

When the soldiers swung the hammer, the galaxies all swirled.

The light of God's love shone through the world and the hammer.

God knew such a simple tool and His only Son could make such a clamor.

We are like a hammer — a part in the story God has planned.
Shining light into this world while placed in His everlasting hand.
We can't do it on our own. He helps us swing with might.
Trusting Jesus is our only hope to make this world shine bright.

About the Author

KATIE JO HOOK is a graduate of Murray State University (Murray Kentucky), where she double majored in Elementary Education and Special Education. She grew up as a preacher's kid and lived in a ministry where she saw the grace of Jesus Christ change lives. After teaching special education and having three children of her own, God is continuing to use her life to tell people about Jesus. www.katiejohook.com

About the Illustrator

NATHAN CORBIT is an artist native to Southern Illinois. He received his bachelor's degree in art education at Southern Illinois University and his master's degree from the University of Nebraska. He lives in a small community with this wife and three children. Along with making art, he also teaches at the local school. In his free time, he enjoys being with family, painting, photography, hiking, running, and biking.

CPSIA information can be obtained
at www.ICGtesting.com
Printed in the USA
BVHW091432250919
559367BV00023B/953/P